GW00336074

Under A Mind's Staircase

First published 2021 by The Hedgehog Poetry Press

Published in the UK by
The Hedgehog Poetry Press
5, Coppack House
Churchill Avenue
Clevedon
BS21 6QW

www.hedgehogpress.co.uk

ISBN: 978-1-913499-22-8

A CIP Catalogue record for this book is available from the British Library.

Under A Mind's Staircase

by

Robin McNamara

Contents

SINS OF SOULS

Inspired by T.S. Eliot's,
The Love Songs of J. Alfred Prufrock

Indeed there will be a time,
I dare to eat a peach of a poem,
There will be scurrilous looks and frowns
Upon judgmental brows, as time chimes
The coming of the secretive hour and
Peaches of seduction, ripened and seedless.
A virgin tastes this forbidden fruit of lust.
(And how they will be consumed)
Town windows are hushed shut by curtains,
That drape over voyeuristic impulses.
The sins of souls bourne out of shame
Are shared in confession to the Father.
The three Hail Marys, somehow conjure:
A fruitless redemption.

THE DEVIL'S LIST

(Inspired by Mikhail Bulgakov's novel,
The Master and Margarita)

Demon dogs howl at the moon's rise.
The room is readied with incense of
    Frankincense and myrrh.

Have the angels fled?

A shadowy figure moves slowly;
Almost elevated.

The grass is scorched from hooves
    Of the called.

As the devil thrills a captive audience,
With his splendid playing of the violin.

'Such gusto! Bravo sir!'
    — How the fires are stroked.

Such glow cast upon faces.
'Care for a margarita?' To watch the burning

Of the Testament.

For the poet hasn't arrived yet with a rebuttal.
Dare he try? He lays at the Devil's
Feet—   like a faithful dog.

The crowds dance like mistresses
To music of the Devil's symphony.

Have the angels fled?

The sounds cascade down their writhing bodies-
The fiddle has them captivated.

It's inside them/possesses them.
    How they moan...

In a dream-like state, the music of the
Stradivarius wraps its trilled
embrace round me.

The angels have fled.

EVOLVED-DARWINISM

In metaphysical terms, how do you
Seek out the God that's worshipped
From the ground, to a higher level?
Are the actions of a lesser man worth
The attention of a gold and silvered religion?
Does the mind evolve its thoughts or
Scientific understanding in a lifetime,
Just like the metamorphosis of an insect,
Evoking evolution's cycle?
A Darwinian inheritance: an existential acceptance
Of evolutionary biology.
How the gilded gates of conformity open up
Only to an acceptable few.
Those who catch the existence of life/
Their hands cupped 'round a moulded theory,
Carefully taken from corpses of theological minds.
Broken species long gone to extinction.
Rest.

BLACKBIRD ON THE HILL

During a frosted morning walk,
When my breath hung as cold vapour
And fingers become numb to touch,
There perched a blackbird on a hill—
Poised upon a rickety farmer's fence,
In dignified stillness.

The blackbird plucked the briars and brambles,
Pregnant with blackberries. It matters not to me,
The myths they provoke, nor the foretelling of their presence,
As long shadows traced the telling of an impending
Arrival of a late guest. Dusk readied as I walked
Towards the blackbird on the hill.

THREE GRAMS OF SUGAR

A sugar cube weighs,
Three grams.
Your sweetened lies,
Weigh the same as
A sugar cube.

Bitter sweetness
Dissolves on my tongue,
Deception lurks in the corners of your eyes
Deep eyes of deception,
As black as the untouched/ cold coffee.

Your love dissolves,
Like a three gram sugar cube.

REGRESSION

Here comes the rain
With evening's darkness.
In creeps the night
With its malevolent eye.

How long will day's brightness
Remain ----

Before the crow's flight?
In clouds, oh I die

And fall to ground
Like stones of hail,
Apricity of the Sun,
Fleeting.

Distressed beats
Of wings, so frail.
Ah now, I will regress.

WHO MAY I SAY I AM TODAY?

Those foreboding walls
Of your enclosure.
Did a dead man's tale
Bring the future failure
Before conformity?
Let the lesions linger
For they hum out the worded pain:
You spoke to evoke a new happening.
Clarity whispers seductive
Afterthoughts - as the poet
Looks the book and wears
The accepted clothes.

THE BATTLE OF MOYTURA

Death has come and death has gone,
The lush cailín no longer sings her song.
The final swoop of the Mór-ríoghain above
Crimson scarred lands; barren of
Life, barren of victory. The shadowed passage
Between the living and the otherworld
Is fudged. The final swish of swords/of shields
Clanging and screams reverberating
Across the valley has died to a single whisper/
Guttural sound.
The lonely *kraa* of the crow
Above Mór-ríoghain watches ghosted
Souls cross into the afterlife.

ROUGH

In marked twain the sunlight left.

The night took over the sleeping hills.
Foreclosed the light of day,

Resting the fields from a day's drought/
A day's thought.

Bedrock stone unrounded
And unground.

Who thought the waters' flow

And the waters gone
Would shape your roughing?

Cold to the touch and
Cold to the palm.

SOUL OF DUST

*"I will show you fear
in a handful of dust."*
T.S. Eliot

The fire went out:
Your extinguished life no more than dust
In the palm of another hand.
The extinction of all of you.

What will anything matter in time?

The ashes of your flesh and bones
That encased your soul
Released into the winds
Along with lost dreams.

The weight of a body/armour
The ribbed cage of a heart,
Gone to dust.

What will it matter in time?

PRESSED FOR TIME

When the winds rustled through
The yellow fields of corn,

I thought of a safe place.
A place I'll return to with
Grey hair and creaking bones.

Hours of time spent in this old rocking chair,
Aged by history,

Its rhythmic creaks sound
Across the golden-lit porch;

Sun's dying light strives
To remain relevant to the current day.

Alas, like all things in life, it must
Come to its ending. The light—
Pressed for time—quickly departed.

TIDES AND SEASONS

It was always there, the calling,
In the silence of briars in meadows
That covered the bloom of heather
And life unseen, in noise of rushed life.
Oh, the sounds of waves that crash the rocks
That jutted up in defiance.
Pebbles applause for the returning
Tides.

It was always there, the calling,

In the noise of choirs in shadows
Of swallows that come together,
In nested trees, in this wildlife.
Though, the weeds bloom and mock
The garden's elegance, they shoot up
In defiance.
Rebels of nature for the returning
Seasons.

APPLE PICKING SEASON

In morning's softness, wispy fog swirls
Around the apple trees, ripe for the picking.
Fruit nestled like red earrings on holly green,
Glistening with the morning dew.

Although some had fallen to ground,
Ruined with brown, I began the apple picking.
The ripest ones first. I held the harvest
In my hands, a spectrum of red, this Adam
And Eve fruit and its promises of sweetness
For the season.

DUSKED EVENINGS

When
Shadows hang upon the horizon,
Meadows yawn in dandelions
That call the bees to suckle
Their nectar: sweetness on a
Summer's evening. Hedgerows
Release their perfume scents.
My senses are intoxicated with
Herbaceous fragrance.
The sun lies slyly on the sleeping horizon.
When I was once a countryside boy,
This was summer.

THE FROSTED EYE

Your frosted eye lingered
Upon an extinguished candle.
Ice-cold breath,
The memories of us repressed
Like a long ago death;
Like winter trees undressed.

Your frosted breath lingered
On the windowpane.
You enhanced the sorrow
Of our time long-forgotten.
You promised a false tomorrow
The hymns of our love begotten.

Your frosted touch lingered
Long after departure.
You evaporated like a guilty mistress,
No longer here do you belong.

MAYBE WE'LL BE AMAZED

Maybe we'll be amazed.
Maybe we'll be amazed somehow
In this amazing sun?
Seductive corona on the rim
Of a day gone / a day spent.

Fade away, fade away into the past.
The light — never lasting
After the sun drops
In the darkness' maze.
Here we go, here we go again,
Things like love are —
Interspersed.

Maybe we'll be amazing
Together, lost in the dark
With this something:
This...appetency
For something more.
Our religion's stopped keeping score
A long time ago.

LOBSTERLAND

Like a fish out of water,
I'm living in Lobsterland,
Near the Butter mountains.
Surreal is the new normal:
Nobody stares and I'm going
To live forever, without breathing
Your toxicity,
Pollution or rabid mouth.
It's all a great misinterpretation of life.
But it doesn't matter because
I'm living in Lobsterland,
Where I'll never be red or dead.

MUSE

Can you shape a melody,
That shows how I see you
In blue: sweet, strumming.

I guess you were always around,
Like raindrops, teasing my thirst.
Don't you want to understand?

I promise that you do,
Your dreams gone
In the morning dew,
As you shape a melody
For the world and you.

ALICE IN UNDERGROWTH

Slithery, slimy snakes and snails,
Wriggling, crawling, slimming across
The forest floor undergrowth.

Nibbling magic mushrooms, giggling like
Alice in Wonderland.

Buttercups, teacups, all thrive here
In the undergrowth of the poet's imagination.

Robert Frost, lost in woods by a road in the undergrowth.
(Seriously!)

No time to waste, *run rabbit run*!
The lichen and moss grows
Slowly over my mind.

DUBLIN

This poem is inspired by
Stephen James Smith's Dublin You Are.

Dublin: fair city, you always were
And always will be the eye of Ireland
With the seagulls perched on the top
Of Liberty Hall on Eden Quay.
With a birds-eye view of
Daily hustle.

On Saturdays, the birds sit atop
Clery's clock, watching first dates,
Whilst the dancing lady waltzes by.
Dancing Mary, giz a twirl.
And who remembers the Diceman,
With his flirty winks on Grafton Street?

Dublin: fair city, you always were
And always will be the eye of Ireland.
Newly arrived from the countryside, such
Vibrancy and warmth of the Dubs.
Fish and chips from Leo Burdocks? Yes, please!
The coddle, you can keep.

O'Connell Street, where's your identity gone?
Fast food for fast lives. Did we change from
Sackville Street for this?
Don't forget the poets hidden by books
In the Winding Stair bookshop. Bring back
Ulysses, Dublin you are: me.

THE SCHOOL TEACHER

It wasn't you I hated,
Just the click of the chalk
On the blackboard.
Your monotone voice,
As you recited the formula,
Like a priest giving his sermon.
The maths equation was
The nemesis to my creativity,
Which was strangled by a
School tie I wore
In a dull, grey building,
In a small town, with my unproven
Unborn ability.

To the class in Irish after Maths,
You, oh, Christian Brother,
Poured me some misery,
About the life of Peig Sayers,
In a language foreign to me,
Because of an 800-year history.
I didn't hate you, just
The woman in the book, her
Life forced upon me.
I, behind the desk I did not own ,
In a dark, grey building
Of ties and bored faces
And an ancient language
We'd never use in daily life.

Nor did I hate the examiner
In the hall, looking down,
With a frown at my half-empty,
Page of answers to questions,
I had no inclination to care about,
In this grey building of school ties.

The daily grinds of after school
Did deliver the desired acceptance,
That my school life served a purpose,
But showed me no directions, nor clarity.
I walked away with no glance back;
Tall, dark, grey building with those,
Nameless unestablished faces.

Monotone-voiced teachers,
Stare blankly at new faceless potentials,
Who've taken our places as they,
Once again, turn to the blackboard,
And write with chalk their boredom,
In mathematical formulas.

THE NUN ON THE BICYCLE

(Based on a true story)

I met a nun cycling an old bicycle
I told her I loved the decrepit thing,
She said:
 "It takes me quicker to God...
But I could do with a new one."
I told her I religiously collected old bicycles,
So she said:
 "You buy me a new one and you
Can have my old bicycle."
I said:
"It's a deal."
So I bought her a new bicycle;
Shiny and quick.
We both won and got to our respective
Religions faster.

THE FOLD OF THE SEASONS

When the ceremonial falling began,
With the departure of the leaves
This fallen October,
The red-brick terraced homes
Light the first fires.
Wisps of smoke
Permeate the crisp air.
People hunched over with work and worry
Shuffle past.
The colours of the seasons will soon
Wear their monochrome coats of rest.

HAPPILY EVER AFTER

In this house of ours,
We (*you*) picked out

The new wallpaper in this
Sitting room of silence.

The pictures on the wall
In the hallway near the door

(Which once promised freedom)

Seems somewhat... incongruous,
To what the separate bedrooms
Entails.

Two unfulfilled souls in their
Own Les Misérables.

Frowns, sighs and shrugs
Are reiterated daily.

From blossoming beginnings:

"You're so lovely!"
"Ah stop, I'm blushing!"

To the happily ever after of:

"Did you put the bloody bin out?"
"Where's my socks?"

AUTOPSY OF A WRITER

You reached in
And pulled out
My beating heart -
As if the dismemberment
Wasn't enough
Of the limbs that walked me
Safe from those judges.
My blood flowed crimson
Across rejected pages of torn poetry,
Abandoned and burnt
Like a witch at the stake.

Here were the remains of any creativity:
Your fingers probed; crushed my brain
The creative left side
'Till it mulched under your criticism.

No more verses
No more judgement
And no more poet.

GARDEN OF LIFE

When the feeble wind blows
The ghosts sway,
But never go away;
Only to remain inside of me.
The leaves sway on trees
To remind me
Seeds were once sown
And dreams were once grown,
From my hands and from yours,
We'd planted some hope.
We had all the love to help us cope
For a time, in our little garden
Of life.

The boats sway but never go away
We sail to a land we promised ourselves
Away from a broken heartland
And strife.
Will you sit by me?
Listen to the greatest hits we
Played together.
C'mon now, here comes the sunset,
Closing the curtains on all our
Missed opportunities.
All grey and wrinkled—
(I'm still young inside, for fucks sake!)
Perhaps you believe in reincarnation?
Perhaps...

IT'S QUITE MENTAL, REALLY

Like a depressed version of
Rodin's Sculpture, *The Thinker*-

I'm hunched up, mind unfolding:
Out escapes everything.
Fear, anxiety and phobias
S c a t t e r.
I almost trip over my
Arachnophobia in haste to
Escape my coulrophobia.
It's no joke really-

That... film, I can't watch *IT.*
And that song, *99 Red Balloons?*

Definitely can't listen to that.
I tried to take a walk but-

My Agoraphobia said,
"I'm back bitch."

So the black dog started
To whine incessantly,

Inside my head.
And yep, you've guessed it-

My phobia: cynophobia did
Not helping matters *at all.*

Now I've gone barking mad.

NO MAN'S ISLAND

I'm an island unknown/
Unexplored by discoverers.

No feet embed the sands,
Nature is undisturbed.

No one hears the waterfalls
Nor the free-running rivers.

I'm an island undiscovered,
I've had no visitors, only

Birds of paradise that rest
In nests of tropical trees.

Unblemished and unseen
My geography is unmapped.

I'm an island uninhibited
By settlers, by pirates,
No tribes have rowed

The sapphire waters
To my shore in conquest.

I am an island alone/
No man's Island.